BLUE BAROMETERS

AYNI

Blue Barometers

R. A. MAITRE

PETERLOO POETS

First published in 1986
by Peterloo Poets
Treovis Farm Cottage, Upton Cross, Liskeard, Cornwall PL14 5BQ

ISBN 0 905291 76 X

Printed in Great Britain by
Latimer Trend & Company Ltd, Plymouth

ACKNOWLEDGEMENTS are due to the editors of the following publications in which some of these poems first appeared: *Country Life, The Countryman, Other Poetry, Outposts Poetry Quarterly, Poetry Matters, Poetry Review.*

"The Combines" won a £100 prize in the 1982 National Poetry Competition, and was read by the author on *Poetry '82* (BBC Radio 3).

Cover illustration: by Barry Camp.

Photo of author: by Ben Coveney Harris

For Doreen, with love

Contents

POSTCARDS FROM NORTH NORFOLK

Blakeney

An anchor shape in flint by a quayside
beneaped on the marshes, here colonies
of the elderly, retired military
men in yachting caps and anoraks, broad-

in-the-beam spouses in lisle stockings,
slowmarch the cobbled streets, *The Times*
under their arms like swagger canes,
in tow sometimes, a debby offspring,

tight-bummed in blue denim, hippy feet,
lippy looks—chicks who sail too near the wind
with guys in London. They need the rest . . .

Boats jigger and bob on the jetty;
clouds jill along; yellow rivulets drain
a sun stuck in the putty.

Cley-next-the-Sea

It's Sunday. 7 a.m. Not a soul about.
That sense of space prepared for another.
Horses crop a scoured meadow
next a patch of gulls like mushrooms sprouted

overnight. A church on the rise
eyes a blind sea under a veil.
On the green, more gulls
strut in phalanx, cacophonise

bleary air, make early-morning calls
no one wants, parade the ground of pantiles.
But the trees are spruce, up and about

long before figures stalk Sundays, cigarettes,
obedient church bells chime when tolled,
clouds lower for the heavens to unfold.

Cley Beach

A long shingle-bank shows where the sea lies,
just beyond it but invisible
till mounted. Seen from sundry miles,
it focuses our walking, a table-

top of land we aim at. The sea's swell's
in our bones, files us across
marshes hardy sheep graze,
patched cows in amiable herds amble.

Today a few odd digits notch the skyline;
vanish as we substitute, take in
the sea's December blues—and a vignette:

a girl skinning legs of fur boots
to paddle with a youth in a greatcoat, their
laughter bleached through sun-brazed air.

Sheringham

No piers here, but a sandy beach,
stout breakwaters defending it.
Wintering, the sands lack feet,
prints of countless toes that etch

fine grains in Summer. The prom
lacks waves of strollers, pink
rock-shops shut, one-armed bandits
paralysed with boredom.

Undeflected, the beaches stretch
east the few miles to Cromer,
black-wracked groynes in the dimmer
light of dawn or evening, coal silhouettes

feinting a visual art.
The telescope takes a solipsistic view.
In Summer, its suction cap glues
eyes to girls half-clad, mixed fruits

variously appealing: a little peach
plump in tie-sides; bottoms'
pyriform swell in skins
wrinkled on dimpling cheeks;

pouched breasts lugged like pomegranates;
and, melting like a lolly,
a fleeting beauty's
lemon, Lurex swimsuit

in a kaleidoscope of synthetics
on sands now threadbare,
uncandystriped by clashing chairs
dealt like cards from decks.

Weybourne Beach

Beached boats and bits of iron on shingle mounds
weed patches anchor in. Behind, angular fields
tractors engage. Gulls on circular tours.
Ships' glints remote. A sky that flares

to catch the sun sloping off over
cropped sandhills an edged wind strops and shears.
Bellied dunes that shiver.
Tree hunchbacks. A few strollers

dot these shingles,
buttoned up against the easterlies,
crunch the pumiced pebbles

with dogs, frisking unleashed, mewed
barks melded with wind yelp—then
muffled as a jet flight hugs the coastline,

westing, Harriers on the wing.
Miles out,

sea and sky are quietly wedding.

Coastlines

A bleak coast this—and forgotten.
It's as though years don't matter
when you reach the sea,
its shores bare of habitation

along miles of shingle. Only
skylined winking ships
remind one of the century—
and in Summer, the girl who slips

off her clothes to bathe
in three triangles of nylon.
Now the days

draw in, vectored on
December, a solstitial glow
that sets this place in light to hallow.

A COLLEGE LIFE

Quad

December. We spend the term's last weeks
quadrangled by the short day.
Across frosted grass, students make their way
to tutorials or coffee breaks.

Some waning afternoons,
an apricot sunlight is quintessential,
our diminutive rooms seem umbral
hides where no real light has shone,

we don the guise of luminaries,
stuffy beings whose inner lights are snuffed.
I watch the sun huffed

by clouds and skyline, twilit
ghosts skid ice for a sunflower doorway,
split Aristotle for hedonistic light.

Dialogue

The weeks draw on. Light is tapered,
in its distillation, Plato taught,
the ghost of Socrates caught
in this cuboid room, blurred

shapes and shades of orchids in a sky
that's mute beyond a vocal class.
Euthyphro and *Protagoras*
occupy us, the question why

"virtue" is so refractory.
I smile inwardly,
knowing the intractable territory,

marking my own inconsistency
in matters of love. I'd bed you
if you'd have me ... Sweet sophistry ...

Issues

Vitelline sun illuminates the table;
under our loupe, the "aesthetic";
through glass, December's hermetic
glaze, the tack of sable

clouds through a daffodil sky—
unnoticed as we draw on cigarettes,
fingers trace the Braille dots
on mugs of Nescafé,

our constructs flare and fade
like the sun through a pane that squares
its plum circle,

each draw on thought we exhale
so much mist on glass
fuzzing a *bricoleur's* landscape.

Abstraction

That life of contemplation Plato taught,
we imitate. I write a book on art's
concept. Yet my heart's
not wed purely to celibate thought:

I stray beyond the print's crisp pica,
analyse floral curtains
where dull girls shine
at intercourse. And the flicker

of April sun through filtering limbs
trips me through years of bent-back study
to woodland rides where we

scanned the leafing elms
for the dip and glide of the White Admiral:
metamorphic time, scaled by the ephemeral.

Knowledge

I err—willingly! Sweet *akrasia!*
It should not have been,
but now, between
institution sheets, brief ambrosia

leased from the gods. Her parents overlook
our act from their photograph; the clock
marks time; a sock
blackmarks the carpet; the twist and crook

of cast stockings sloughed in haste,
and triangles of underwear
antimacassar a chair.

And when it's done I stroke her hair,
note how the sun fingers a breast
before it dips below a gable's crest.

Assessment

The years accumulate; blur
in vapid memory, conflated, half-discrete.
Only their locus, this quad, where this year's feet
mark a new time, is clear.

And I veer: a pendulum swung between
my ingrained way of desk and book,
the habit of abstraction a crook
I'm comfortable in,

and some *via negativa*. And the beat
of a proximate heart,
scented femineity,

effloresce with peaks' nebulous promise;
while sunlight saps my work's premise,
disclosing my books: limp, dusty.

COUNTRY LIFE

The Tractors

Day in, day out, they
rasp and judder
up and down the lane,
cheery headphoned drivers

inured to rough rides
saddled with diesel horses,
on display in glass cases
like rural specimens,

or down-to-earth pilots
cockpitted, their machines
macho yet curiously gay,
swinging in shades of the 60s

like sherbet-lemon,
dreamy tangerine or
jade green—
glosses that go and

jar with the fields they
surf on distantly,
gulls in their wake as they
tow steel ploughshares.

In close-up, they're
jerky, tensed creatures,
jittery bonnets arabesqued in mud;
fume as their voice-boxes

blare out riffs of heavy metal.
At night they're parked
higgledy-piggledy in the farmyard,
where they ruminate

like a space-age breed of cattle—
to the strutting hens
who scrape and sift under them,
taciturn giants eminently gentle.

The Combines

Combines whine from deeps in the ochroid fields,
their motors pitched like angry insects.
Paired, they cross at intervals,
lolly green on green. A tractor's

strawberry marks time; then moves at a signal
to match a combine's pace and line,
cart catching the husky gush from a funnel.
They look conjoined like planes refuelling.

Their harvesting spans the dry days
as Summer wanes and Autumn takes command.
Stubble-smoke billows scent the air with bonfire,
mar afternoon brightness with premonition,

and shorn fields bear black stripes like pelts.
They drone deep into evening,
often homing under moonlight,

looming out of the fields with mounting
stridence, large-headlighted, like space invaders.
Passing, they rivet us. Even the ground shudders.

The Fields

We are encircled by fields,
the ground of our living here.
They stretch to thin chinked belts
of shadowy copses, trees' particular

laceworks. Like an endless chameleon,
their tones adapt to the seasons,
even when lying fallow.
Most are sown, the lone figure

of a plodding tractor in green
or zesty clementine all day
methodically covering ground;
noiseless except when a wave of sound

ripples out to us as a trough is crossed
in the lapped crests of loam
rolling in the distance.

In Summer, barley and wheat coexist
in mellow harmony,
ears cocked in the wind.

Coppices shield them from the easterlies,
filter early light
spilling its glorious honey.

All bee-winged day it gilds the fields' meshed combs.
At night, a silver-top moon
milks them of their ambrosia.

Horse Sense

In milked light, two horses loom,
equine shapes in a paddock that hints of mist
and breathes dampness. They seem
oblivious of what strikes us,

homing down the lane whose ragged hedge
gives us glimpses of them.
They get on with the job of cropping, nudge
a neighbour's dark flank—movement

startling as ghosts. On
the sky-line, traces of rose remain
in a hedgerow of ultramarine,

our own scoured plane—
our megafield framed with dying images,
a sun that ducks and hedges.

Shooting Party

Advance reports of their unseen stalking
thud out sporadically, drumbeats from a copse
across the clodland. A grey day that drips
moribundly till cracks in the clouds' lagging

flicker copper. A sudden
flurry of pheasants in a clutch bat air
distantly, too late, too low to clear
the staccato fusillade shotgunning

into them. Most plump
lifeless the sodden ground.
Then men and black dogs abound,

emerging, a dozen, from the wood, the warp
of remoteness and new silence feinting
the muteness of a pastoral painting.

In Different Lights

1. MORNING

Our view here is unspoilt. Just
fields and trees. Now, in November,
a pocket of mildness, flutters
of wind greet our breakfast;

and a seminal sky clouds
the braze of sunshine
we shall walk in later, the afternoon
burnished and buffed

by dusters of haze muffling distance.
Now light's restrained, latent
with what's to come—more

than sun or solstice:
some immanence seems to grace us
as we sweep leaves, saw logs for the fire.

2. EVENING

Barrows on the common. Six tumuli.
Graves amongst the gorse. The slight
tumescence of dim ages. A family
gone to ground and become it. Light

from a moribund sun gives perspective.
I march on brackened earthworks
a scant mile away on a massive
scarp, totter on its apex,

overlook land draining
of sharpness, humps and hollows,
crests and forests merging.

Dark, as in a barrow's bowels,
it is—except for the stars that pip
a colander sky with escape routes.

Mists

A mist hangs all day, snuffs
sky and metal skyline;
a subjunctive's ifs
and buts shelve sunshine.

And a curious silence buffs
active voice and traffic
as though mist's concept imposed it:
a world of bluff

where throttling cars are mute or purr,
crisp vocals are stifled
as though Design rifled
sounds of all vibrant burr.

A mystic might
discern hints of unworldliness—
atemporal glints.
We—we have to guess.

Thomas

Not long with us, rescued from a pound,
this svelte, milk-bibbed tabby
had spent idyllic days in our poppied
garden basking, the warrened field beyond

stalking rabbit young lolloping,
carrying their limp forms home like a she
kittens; he lapped gold-top like a baby;
unfurled like petals at our fondling.

Then listlessness struck. He spent
hot days and moonbeamed nights in our caravan
as though a hospital he'd recover in.

The last day, Gilbert & Sullivan
played in the car as he, basketed, went
through ripe cornfields musky with grass scent.

Not that he could see, or even cared to smell.
He returned limp as his rabbits. Soft and small.

The Hamlets: Observations on December 25th

From the sea road, the lane up
to these hamlets
suckling in the downs, passed
through a farmyard as the map

predicted. It seemed strange.
So did the hamlets,
rings of stonework set
in the laps of chalky bulges,

the odd light, the scent of woodsmoke
a spare top line
to the downs' infrasonic

bass-rhythms. But in Littlebredy, the rake
of slope alarming where dwellings heeled in,
there hung a question mark:

a few cows eyed us over a gate,
cud-chewing. Otherwise,
nothing but a sea-like sibilance,

the calcium light these hill-loaves
steeped in. A track pocked
with flints fissured a backlit dome.
Where we stopped, trees checked

sunlight with jigsawing boughs,
lane and cottages patched
with dapples brilliantly aped by the cows.
Through interstices, eyes watched . . .

Winter Time

The coal fire in the sky's
beyond stoking;
three mallards flee
the ennui of a living-room wall.

Trimphones still ring in the woods
where hen birds scuttle about,
shutting up for night.
A geometry

of graphic electric lights
advertises a frosty distance
tucked across the fields—

the anachronistic stuff of Christmas cards
where the church clock's pump-clank chimes
still mark time.

Tooth & Claw

Corrosion on brass . . . Covens
where rooks flock the sky,
drop in on a

dead oak's charnel house.
The plough has rigor mortis . . .
Passerine cacophony . . .

Then the silence of the grave . . .
Odd sparrow squeaks.
A rabbit shriek,

balletic plump fur
doing a pas de deux
with a flick-knifing stoat.

On a fur cushion,
a hare's bare backbone
honed to the ivory.

Up a cart-track,
the albumen glaze of the mortuary
in puddle-eyes,

claws' broad arrows
plover gangs have unmanacled.
Midfield,

a crucified scarecrow
bows out with hypothermia . . .
Then nirvana:

mist snuffs shifty coppices
where a fox dons sneakers,
gashed clouds haemorrhage.

TRANSPORTS OF ADOLESCENCE

Transports of Adolescence

Roman-straight streets in parallel . . .
Mine butted a pond steam-trains
shushed across, their night rush
sibilant for lampblack miles . . .

On commons, the grumble of manoeuvres,
the chant of crepitant blanks,
my stamping ground the tank tracks
where I exercised dreams of lovers . . .

But our passion was jet-shriek,
sonic booms all airshow week:
the megatonic crack and shudder

as flash Lightnings in a quiver
bombarded the afternoon,
haloed with shimmers of afterburn.

Town & Country

Town. A rude awakening in a clearing:
the barracks of an estate,
satsuma brickwork, stilted car ports,
a landscaped drive dead-ending;

and the dusk flare of sodium,
garish through coppices' fretwork—
yet electromagnetic
as the commonlands' stadium

of ridges and spurs
defected into gunmetal strangeness,
twilight's iron curtain,

town one's domain,
the streets all rote-learnt,
the route to a room,

its window a picture of those heights
still glimmering.

Streets

Pedalling the streets of my hometown,
it's light, air I recall—
aqueous, edged; and the seasons'
inflections on the small

plots I swept past, their
gardens cultivated relations
with a commonland glint in the eye,
their primal leanings

towards the cloudscaped
tracts bare miles about them;
and that rim

of sheened rises vistaed through gates—
blue barometers
glassy with a luminous weather.

Girls

No girlie mags in my day.
Some minor titillation in the tabloids.
But no nudes,
bulbously unclad breast and thigh

come-hithering from erotic covers.
Nor local girls from the bank
shedding their knicks for frank
Ektachrome shots of buttocks and vulva.

Ours was a world of innocence,
nice girls in cotton pants.
Goers wore nylons, and we knew of suspenders

and stocking-tops distantly, dark bars
glimpsed in shady affairs of stooping.
They flagged the danger zones of "heavy petting".

Hillfort

A square-root sign of tableland
familiar as a logo,
its faulty geometry was scaled
in graphic blues,
its crest a toothbrush of pines.

Quiescent promontory,
its eagle eye scanned miles
of Hants and Surrey,
blueprint hill
whose Quinked lines were drawn

up on draughtsman's sheets of sky.
Made for bearings, it swung
magnetically
some needle in me, flung
me towards its Iron Age pole,

its cross-ramparts and ditches,
prehistoric barrows,
as though something of those dim ages
pulsed psychic morse—
ursignals,

that ring of pines
wielding arcane semaphore
to flag us in
across a sea of heath and gorse,
decoy us to an untrue North.

Negative

I could hear a gown-skirt rustling
Before I could see her shape . . .
Thomas Hardy, *On a Heath*

Tanks in abundance,
sappers and armoured cars,
I met—but
never you, the light
of your glance on the commons

outshining the sun's top brass,
your hourglass
in gumboots on the heights
in rooty heather, print skirt
pleated by the winds.

Men only,
pipped and red-bereted,
strutted and leopard-crawled
this blue, cicatrised land,
their khaki

strike-vehicles
filmic on the withers of hills,
while I spoored a yeti
on the ground of stony
negatives of treads and shells.

COLD SHOULDERS

Cold Shoulders

Whatever the reason, it seemed better
to pace the wintry commons,
sketchily composed, drizzled on,
griseous skies' amorphous smother

grey as gasworks, trees thin as rakes,
diaphragmatic; whatever the reason,
better to dog fogged skylines,
breach hermetic woods, stamp dank

bracken, pierce rain mist, anticipating
the serried spurs' loom,
like whales out of the gloom,
a school of hills floating;

better though world leap and bound,
nothing solider were on offer
than these eons-old cold shoulders
of wind-souled ground.

My Father

Today he would have been 73.
My father, born on the 13th and ill
luck starring him all the way.
Son of a chef; from France; R.C.

A fat lot of good the bloody Church did!
And as for brothers . . . Once he painted,
and well: a Packard under trees by a lake,
moonlit, he showed me. Thwarted

in all he attempted, I ask why life
was so unfair to this modest man
whose hopes fruited in cancer, he waif-

like thin in a chest hospital, a strong Spring
he could have painted, shimmering outside,
pregnant as he with the sad death he fathered.

Couples

That shaped smoke that is the skyline
is always there, now
erased by mists, now
smudged by petrol rain,

now salient with detail: the filigree
of a town, fields'
multicoloured labels—
at dusk, a sea

where lights wink seductively,
quilts of stratus slip
off carmine sheets ... It
haunts me

as eyes rove out to foreign rooms
in blueprint towns where
others stare
in similar twosomes,

at that shaped smoke that is the skyline,
is always there, now
erased by mists, now
smudged by petrol rain.

A Modern Thomist

After a strange experience while saying Mass on 6th Dec. 1273, St Thomas Aquinas never wrote again, saying "I cannot, because all that I have written now seems like straw".

He rests, light ailing.
Rays drag their heels across clods.
Potato-drilling
was done last week as he planted

words on fallow sheets,
the tractor's line after
plodding line a match for his own neat
longhand characters—

and the lines on his forehead.
He reads analogy into everything,
some numinous thread
tying the whole of Creation.

Steeped in Aquinas, the fields'
closeness makes him think of straw.
Stubble-burning yields
visions of hellfire,

a green curate's agonies ...
The soubrette
in his one and only diocese,
whose immodest, Summer shorts

billed and cooed "sex"
as she chatted to him
about the new, embroidered vestments,
or his last sermon.

He watched her womanhood swell
and plump in corseting jeans,
ride come-on high heels,
flesh out nylons.

Her confessions settled it . . .
He clutched at his breviary
as, one dark night,
she appeared naked in the vestry . . .

Now evenings hammer most:
the bloodless wine on the land,
silver hairs of mist . . .
And Doubt spans

whole nights of mortality . . .
The unuttering universe,
his cerebral harvest's paucity,
bedrooms' sly ambers . . .

Hearses

They're in no hurry,
don't give a monkey's about tailbacks,
deadlines of Routemasters,
a supercilious crew in top hats,
corpse-still Charons in Daimlers,
their updated ferries.

They stick out a mile—
like London-to-Brighton vintage cars—
in their spit-and-polished bootblack,
slow-marching convoys
with a pine-look box in the back,
putting on the style.

Once old timers raised their caps,
women drew respectful curtains,
crossed themselves in that
sudden darkness at noon.
Now they're matter-of-fact,
swallow perhaps,

glimpsing the way of all flesh
past chippy and Chinese takeaway,
The Cock and its TOPLESS NITE,
Kingdom Hall's rubricated JUDGEMENT DAY,
perishables with a sell-by date . . .
Ash

on an undertaker's arm
is dusted off as, hatless, they dole
out fags by the cars,
meditate on Angel (page-3 girl),
dead to the Muzaky bars
of the 23rd Psalm.

Dodging The Toad

In memoriam Philip Larkin

I dodge the toad whenever I can,
being one of those men
who live on their wits:
pundits,

chatshow folk, touts,
gigolos, clerihewists.
It wouldn't suit me, being a clerk,
getting up in the wintry dark

to commute
in a *Hepworths* suit,
up and down those lines to the city,
five days a week to infinity . . .

each day the same,
tripping points through Clapham,
rubbing shoulders with brokers
and rubber-eyed bridge fours;

bum to bum,
in the Underground scrum,
with *Woman's Own* secretaries,
computerised actuaries.

Not for me, the swift half and pork pie,
the roving eye
clocking pantihose on bar stools,
stocking-tops under tables;

the executive case, its memos,
its bulge of *Playboys* . . .
Think of being them!
Ruled by the alarm,

the in-tray and telephone call,
the typist's unmentionables . . .
Think of being them, sad cameos
on yellow train-windows

when the lights come on at four
at the end of another year.
No, give me your arm, old toad;
I'd break it if I could!

MORE POSTCARDS

Aldershot

A garrison town, drill lines of barracks
everywhere, it wakes
to the distant dog-barks of sergeant-majors
carrying across playing-fields.

As well as the *NAAFI* it has cinemas,
a railway station, a bus terminus,
a prominent gasworks,
tin drum next to the floodlit football-ground.

Sappers, civvied and uniformed, abound,
decoyed by the garish lights
of the amusement arcade,
its moth-clutter of girls outside.

They parade in miniskirts,
regulation high-heels sloped like arms, tight
sweaters medalled with nipples.

The streets are like crisscross webbing.
They rise from the ranks of the town's buildings
to an outcrop of crew-cut hills,

purple at dusk where, sometimes,
a browtop figure's dot

is posted like a lookout.

Barkway

From across the whistling wheat-fields,
it is its rank of council houses
we notice first—like forward defences,
a long line of pillboxes.

Then the head of the square church-tower
in a greatcoat of trees at 2 o'clock.
Stone-grey, it is still the secular
soul of the village, renouncing the traffic

of the High Street for its yewed,
grass-mound graveyard,
stone wall, and facing duck-pond.

Dark and light both paint
patches on the lane's tarmac.
They hint of sermons. It is a place of rest

on close Summer days, cooed there
by ghostly doves; lilted to by water.

Dorset

In the heart of Dorset,
a wrestler's brawn of upland:
the Hardy domains. To the north, a vast
adversary of land is flattened,

expires in a panoramic distance ...
To the south, sometimes
the glint of an eye of sea,
set in the cheeked hills' physiognomy.

The bare metal of a ridgeroad
saddles the hills' broad shoulders.
Little, here,

in the way of dwelling—
little but down after down swelling
under a cloud-sloped sky.

A few villages flock the hillsides
like sheep sheltering from the winds.

Weymouth

Brightonish, it has a long French curve
of sandy beach, a broad esplanade
with cocked-hat seats like mini bandstands,
traffic ever on the march

past the parade line of hotels
(the ubiquitous GRANDS and GRESHAMS),
the flash amusement halls,
garish like teddy boys' socks.

Nearby, the ferry terminal
where a double-funnelled SEALINK steamer,
in patriotic colours, appears
among the facades like a trompe l'oeil.

Out at sea, a long submarine of jetty
points the way to Cherbourg;
ship-shapes slip across the bay.

On the prom, a small Big Ben in maroon,
straight out of Dali,
commemorates Victoria's jubilee.

It clocks the trippers' passing,
Budmouth belles in saucy postcard scenes,

bent couples who watch the sands run out.

Reed

Arable flat, it seems all field and green,
its estate an intrusion in farmland.
Only the old high street, its
few thatched cottages, look right;

and the jumbled farmyard,
the upright John Deere tractors,
the mammoth Klaas harvester,
gleams of Autumn in its headlight eyes.

Tucked away is the expected church,
Norman grey and gritty,
a higgledy-piggledy graveyard
complete with three-line obituaries.

Everywhere, the fields stretch away
to remote, neat coloured parcels
in wrappings of brown and green,
rape's shocking electric melon.

In the fields about us, a few aged oaks,
leafless all year, sketch
maps of deltas; odd telegraph poles
are stabbed in like cocktail sticks.

And over to the east, a silver
tracking-tower tramples the wheat,
a gangly robot,
head in the clouds, reading saucers.